WILD ABOUT CATS!

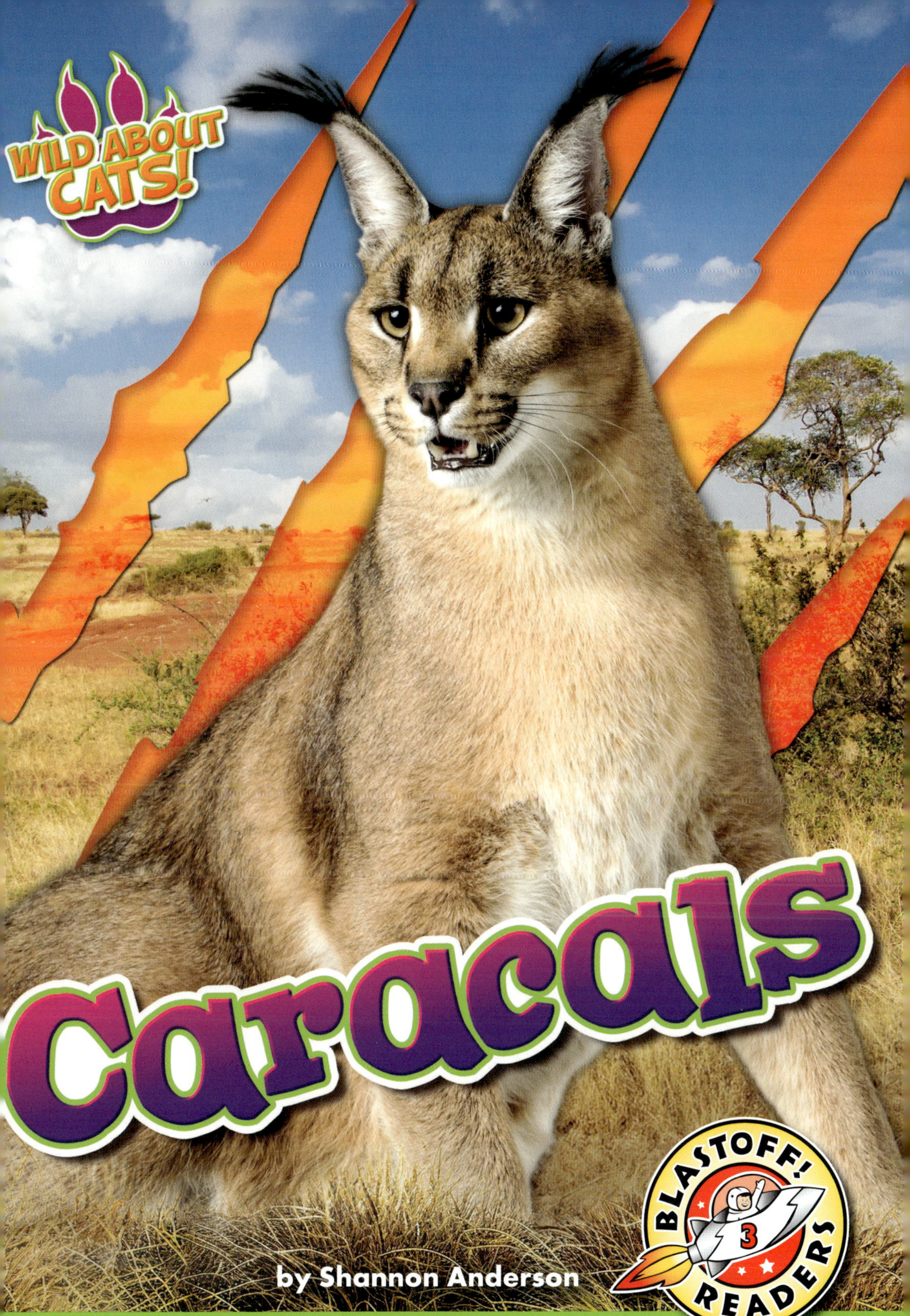

Caracals

by Shannon Anderson

BLASTOFF! READERS 3

BELLWETHER MEDIA • MINNEAPOLIS, MN

Blastoff! Readers are carefully developed by literacy experts to build reading stamina and move students toward fluency by combining standards-based content with developmentally appropriate text.

LEVELS

Level 1 provides the most support through repetition of high-frequency words, light text, predictable sentence patterns, and strong visual support.

Level 2 offers early readers a bit more challenge through varied sentences, increased text load, and text-supportive special features.

Level 3 advances early-fluent readers toward fluency through increased text load, less reliance on photos, advancing concepts, longer sentences, and more complex special features.

★ **Blastoff! Universe**

Reading Level

Blastoff! Beginners — Grade K → Blastoff! Readers — Grades 1–3 → Blastoff! Discovery — Grade 4

This edition first published in 2025 by Bellwether Media, Inc.

Library of Congress Cataloging-in-Publication Data

LC record for Caracals available at: https://lccn.loc.gov/2024046810

Editor: Suzane Nguyen Designer: Brittany McIntosh

Printed in the United States of America, North Mankato, MN.

Table of Contents

Desert Cats

Caracals are known by many names including **desert** lynx. People once trained the cats to hunt animals.

The cats live in many **habitats**, including **savannas** and **grasslands**.

Most caracals live in central and southern Africa. They are also found in parts of Asia.

The number of caracals in the wild is dropping. Habitat loss and hunting harm the cats.

Pointy Ears

Caracals have short, reddish-brown fur. Long, black **tufts** stick out from their pointy ears.

Caracals have long back legs. They can jump over 10 feet (3 meters) high.

Identify a Caracal

Caracals are up to 4 feet (1.2 meters) long. Their tails are about 1 foot (0.3 meters) long.

Size Comparison

house cat	caracal
height at shoulder	**height at shoulder**
around 10 inches (25 centimeters)	around 18 inches (46 centimeters)
length (without tail)	**length (without tail)**
around 18 inches (46 centimeters)	up to 48 inches (122 centimeters)

Females weigh up to 35 pounds (16 kilograms). Males weigh up to 44 pounds (20 kilograms).

Sneaky Night Hunters

Caracals hunt at night.
Great hearing helps them find **prey**. Thick fur on their feet helps them quietly **stalk**.

These cats sometimes chase prey. They take down prey with bites to the neck.

Caracals are **carnivores**. Their favorite foods include hares and birds. They sometimes hunt **livestock**.

The cats even hunt bigger animals like gazelles. They sometimes hide food in trees to eat later.

Caracal Diet

Cape hares

Barbary partridges

dorcas gazelles

Caracal Kittens

Caracals spend most of their time alone. When they have babies, females spend time with their kittens.

They usually have two to three kittens. The babies open their eyes after ten days.

kitten

Females travel with their babies. Young kittens hide in logs and caves.

Baby Caracals

name for babies: kittens
time with mom: around 10 months

At around two months old, the kittens can eat meat. Their big teeth grow in after five months.

Caracal kittens stay with their mom for around ten months. Mom teaches them to hunt.

Then the kittens go off to find a **territory** of their own!

In the Wild

habitats:

forests savannas deserts grasslands

conservation status: least concern

Least Concern	Near Threatened	Vulnerable	Endangered	Critically Endangered	Extinct in the Wild	Extinct

population in the wild: unknown
population trend: going down
life span: up to 12 years

Glossary

carnivores—animals that only eat meat

desert—an area of land that gets little rain

grasslands—lands covered with grasses and other soft plants with few bushes or trees

habitats—the places where animals live

livestock—animals raised on a farm such as goats, sheep, and cows

prey—animals that are hunted by other animals for food

savannas—grasslands in warm areas that have few trees

stalk—to hunt slowly and quietly

territory—the land area where an animal lives

tufts—small bunches of fur on top of an animal's ears

To Learn More

AT THE LIBRARY

Klepeis, Alicia Z. *Lions.* Minneapolis, Minn.: Bellwether Media, 2024.

Murray, Julie. *Caracals.* Minneapolis, Minn.: Abdo Publishing, 2023.

Sommer, Nathan. *Black Mamba vs. Caracal.* Minneapolis, Minn.: Bellwether Media, 2024.

ON THE WEB

FACTSURFER

Factsurfer.com gives you a safe, fun way to find more information.

1. Go to www.factsurfer.com.
2. Enter "caracals" into the search box and click .
3. Select your book cover to see a list of related content.

Index

The images in this book are reproduced through the courtesy of: LifetimeStock, front cover (caracal), p. 22; 25ehaag6, front cover (background); Svetography, p. 3; StuPorts, p. 4; Dubrox, p. 5; Hemis/ Alamy, p. 6; Scott Canning, p. 8; Eric Isselee, p. 9; Stu Porter, pp. 10-11; Nynke van Holten, p. 11 (house cat); Martin Mecnarowski, p. 11 (caracal); Imagebroker/ Alamy, p. 12; RichLindie/ Getty Images, p. 13; robertharding/ Alamy, p. 14; slowmotiongli, pp. 14-15; Robert Harding Video, p. 15 (Cape hares); Martin Pelanek, p. 15 (Barbary partridges); Azahara Perez, p. 15 (dorcas gazelles); Petr Masek, p. 16; Ondrej Chvatal, p. 17; gerard lacz/ Alamy, p. 18 (left); Fiona Ayerst, p. 18 (right); Auscape International Pty Ltd/ Alamy, p. 19; Nature Picture Library/ Alamy, p. 20; David Cantrille/ Alamy, pp. 20-21.